THINGS YOU SHOULD ALREADY KNOW ABOUT DATING,

YOU F♥CKING IDIOT

BEN SCHWARTZ & LAURA MOSES

ILLUSTRATIONS BY LAURA MOSES

hachette
BOOKS

NEW YORK   BOSTON

Hachette Books
Hachette Book Group
1290 Avenue of the Americas
New York, NY 10104
hachettebooks.com
twitter.com/hachettebooks

First Edition: October 2017

Hachette Books is a division of Hachette Book Group, Inc.

The Hachette Books name and logo are trademarks of Hachette Book Group, Inc.

The publisher is not responsible for websites (or their content) that are not owned by the publisher.

The Hachette Speakers Bureau provides a wide range of authors for speaking events. To find out more, go to www.hachettespeakersbureau.com or call (866) 376-6591.

LCCN: 2017936870

ISBNs: 978-0-316-46532-8 (trade paperback), 978-0-316-43500-0 (ebook)

Printed in the United States of America

LSC-C

10 9 8 7 6 5 4 3 2 1

THINGS YOU
SHOULD ALREADY KNOW
ABOUT DATING,

YOU
F♥CKING
IDIOT

CONTENTS

INTRODUCTION

Chances are you've been in this situation before: You're on a date. It's going well! Then, suddenly, your date looks at you like you're a fucking idiot and somehow you've blown it. Guess you're going to die alone, right?

NOT IF YOU READ THIS BOOK!

The thing is, you're probably not even sure what went wrong on that date. Was it your clothes? Your jokes? Your palpable loneliness? Who knows—today's dating scene is a mess. We live in a world where it's become easier to have a relationship over the phone than in person. Common courtesies have been replaced by emojis, and feelings are now expressed through GIFs and memes. So it's not a shock you didn't know that you're supposed to WALK YOUR DATE TO THEIR CAR, YOU FUCKING IDIOT! Sure, you're doing great electronically—your text game is on point and your Twitter feed is fire, but we will teach you how to be a considerate human being on a date in REAL LIFE.

This book contains one hundred simple tips to guide you

through hypothetical dating scenarios. Each tip is paired with a discussion between two people to show you how awesome it is when you take our advice—and how shitty it is when you don't. In case words aren't your thing, you'll also find an adorable illustration next to each tip to make the yucky process of fixing your romantic life a little more whimsical!

So do yourself a favor and read this book immediately, and maybe the next time you show up to a date you'll have a fighting chance at not dying alone.

CHAPTER 1

BEFORE THE DATE

Here you are, a lonely dummy who doesn't want to be lonely anymore. You've been on dates and cried through breakups and it all sucks, so what else is there to do but take off your pants and eat some cookies? FUCK THAT! It's time to get up and change your life! No more DMing randoms or texting late-night hookups. You need to go on a date with a real-life human being of substance. But where do you start? How do you ask someone out? What do you wear? Will there be snacks? Take a deep breath… we are about to break it down for you.

Asking Someone Out

1. Call, text, email, DM…it doesn't matter how you ask, just ask.

   Guy: I'd text you. I would never call you. That is so rude.
   Girl: Asking me out over text is rude! Calling feels special.
   Guy: But if I call you, we would have to talk.
   Girl: What do you think we're going to do on the date?
   Guy: This is moving too fast.

2. When you're asking someone out, be clear that it's a date.

Guy: Wanna come over and chill?
Girl: What does that mean?
Guy: Uh, you know...chiiiiiill.
Girl: "Chill" could mean anything. Am I coming over to watch cat videos or am I coming over to plow?
Guy: Wow...ummm...both?

3. The guy doesn't have to ask the girl out. Either of you can do the asking.

Guy: Traditionally, doesn't the guy ask the girl out?
Girl: Times are a-changin', gramps, we have cars that drive
      themselves now. Anyone can ask anyone.
Guy: OK. Then ask me out.
Girl: I don't want to go out with you.
Guy: But...what if I ask *you* out?
Girl: Woof...

The Location

4. Make sure the location isn't right next to you and moons away from them.

> Girl: There's a cool spot around the corner from me. You wanna meet there?
> Guy: Sounds great.
> *(One bus ride, three subway transfers, and a ten-block walk later.)*
> Guy: Let's just be friends.

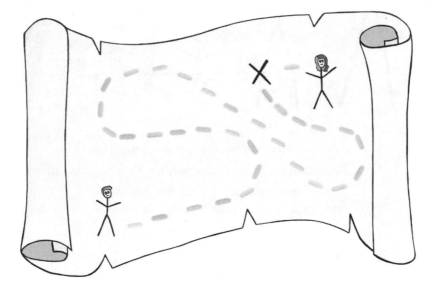

5. Make sure your date spot isn't too trashy or too fancy.

Girl: How much are you going to spend?

Guy: How good that pussy?

Girl: Excuse me?

Guy: I said around forty bucks.

Girl: I thought I heard—

Guy: FORTY. BUCKS.

6. For a first date, start small and meet for a drink.

Guy: We can always upgrade from a drink to a meal if it's going well.
Girl: And if the meal goes well?
Guy: Upgrade to dessert and more drinks!
Girl: And if that goes well?
Guy: Meet my parents and lock it up!
Girl: Really?
Guy: No, you fucking idiot.

7. Make a reservation. You might as well—it doesn't cost any money.

Guy: But it's so embarrassing if I have a reservation and there's nobody in the restaurant.

Girl: Isn't it more embarrassing to be turned away because you don't have a reservation?

Guy: No.

What to Wear/Getting There

8.   Dress like yourself.

Girl: Why are you dressed like James Bond?
Guy: All I have is this or ten pairs of cargo shorts.
Girl: Rethink your entire life.

9. Don't be late.

Guy's text: I'm gonna be fifteen minutes late.
Girl's text: Every minute you're late, I will be on a dating
         app texting someone else.
Guy's text: Be there in two.

CHAPTER 2

ON THE DATE

Holy shit! You did it! You're on a date! There's an actual person sitting in front of you! This is the best part of a relationship because no one has made a mistake yet. But uh oh...this isn't a text conversation. You have to look into someone's eyes and use your mouth words. What do you talk about? What do you order? Do you get super drunk as fast as you can to feel loose and hilarious yet also mysterious? Slow down. Read on.

Drinking and Dining

10. Don't be drunk when you show up for the date.

> Guy: I would never be drunk! That's crazy! Drunk? Dude, you're hilarious! HAHAHAHA! I love how we can just laugh around each other. So chill!
>
> Girl: You're already drunk, aren't you?
>
> Guy: YOU'RE ALREADY DRUNK!!!!!!

11. Don't get too drunk on the date.

Guy: And that was the last time I ever saw my father alive—
Girl: Wait! I love this song!
   (Girl leaps on table.)
Girl: Dance with me!
Guy: I miss you, Dad.

12. Be patient if you're waiting for a table/food/the check.

Girl: Why are you in such a hurry? You better not have
another date, you dick.

Guy: Another date...that's hilarious.

(Guy looks around nervously.)

Girl: Holy shit. Is your next date at this bar?

Guy: Yeah, right! What is this, an eighties sitcom? Let's
get the check.

Girl: That girl is waving to you.

Guy: I'll wave back as a joke.

Girl: I'm out of here.

13. Order food like a full-grown adult. Don't get four baby carrots or seven steaks.

Guy: I'll have a pork chop in between two steaks, please.
Girl: And I'll have a blade of grass, dressing on the side.
(Waiter runs into oncoming traffic.)

14. Be nice to the waiter.

Guy: What if the waiter is bad?
Girl: Try your best to be nice.
Guy: What if the waiter is Hitler?
Girl: Always kill Hitler.

15. If you're a guy on a date with a girl, you're paying. At least for the first date.

Girl: But, like, feminism and stuff.
Guy: I know, but I should pay.
Girl: I make more than you.
Guy: I know. How about you get the next one?
Girl: OK. Thanks.
Guy: Of course...Can I borrow fifty bucks?

Talking and Listening

16. Be real and honest. Don't bullshit someone from the start.

Guy: There's no point in making me fall for a fake you.
Girl: I'm not being fake!
Guy: So you really love *Star Wars*?
Girl: YES.
Guy: Name one character.
Girl: Samuel L. Jackson?
Guy: That doesn't count, he's in everything.

THE GOONIES ARE MY FAVORITE JEDIS!

17. Don't judge someone before you get to know them.

Girl: I Googled you this morning and, honestly, you seem like a dick.

Guy: You can't tell that from the Internet.

Girl: I saw a pic of you drinking a magnum of champagne in a kiddie pool. I'm pretty sure you're a dick.

Guy: That was from a fundraiser where I donated pools to underprivileged orphans. It's my charity. Do you do any volunteer work?

Girl: I…um…

(Girl runs toward the nearest black hole.)

18. Don't just talk about yourself, Kanye. Ask questions and listen.

Girl: Me.
Guy: Me?
Girl: ME.
Guy: ME!
Girl and Guy: MEEEEEEEEEEEEEEEE!!!!!!!!!!!!!

19. Don't bring up your ex on the first date unless they ask. You need to build a bridge before you cross a river of crazy.

Girl: My ex and I used to come here all the time.
Guy: Oh...yeah? Um...did you date for a while?
Girl: SINCEYOUASKED—we dated for twenty-seven weeks. I just think our timing was off and he's really damaged from his parents' divorce, like gun-shy, you know? Also my daddy issues are off the charts so...
(Guy jumps off a bridge.)

20. If you run into someone, introduce them to your date. Don't leave them standing there like a fucking idiot.

Girl: Why didn't you introduce me to that girl back there?
Guy: My bad.
Girl: I was standing there like an idiot the whole time.
Guy: I forgot her name and didn't wanna hurt her feelings.
Girl: You're dating her too, aren't you?
   (Beat.)
Guy: Ummmmmmm... No?

21. Please put your phone down.

Girl: OK, I'll put my phone facedown on the table.

Guy: I can still hear it when you get a text.

Girl: I'll put it on silent.

Guy: Just put it in your purse.

Girl: I can't. My purse is full of...a hundred million tampons.

Guy: You're lying.

Girl: You want me to prove it?

(Girl holds up purse threateningly.)

Guy: No! Fine. Just put it on silent.

CHAPTER 3

AFTER THE DATE

WHO JUST ABSOLUTELY CRUSHED THAT DATE LIKE A PRO?!? YOU DID! Hooray! It's time to walk out of that restaurant with your head high, look your date in the eye, and… and…uhhhh…now what? Should you walk them to their car? Ask them for another date? Attempt the lift from *Dirty Dancing*? OK, first off, stop staring at them like a weirdo and let us help you out.

Saying Goodbye

22. Offer to walk your date to their car/subway/hoverboard after the date.

> Guy: Do you really need me to walk you? You keep going on about how you're strong and independent...and I'm parked in the other direction.
>
> Girl: Stop. No excuses. People are crazy. The world is one big horror movie. Walk me to my car, you fucking idiot.
>
> Guy: Yes, ma'am.

23. Gentlemen, wait for your date's Uber to arrive before leaving in yours.

Guy: What if my Uber shows up first?

Girl: They can wait two minutes.

Guy: I don't want my driver to dock my rating.

Girl: Well, I'd really like the guy I'm with to care more about my safety than his Uber rating.

Guy: I don't know if I can be that guy.

24. If you want to be a hero, pay for their Uber.

>Guy: Let me call you an Uber.
>
>Girl: No, I can do it.
>
>Guy: I got it. It's the app equivalent of me dropping you off
>at home, but with almost no effort on my part.
>
>Girl: You just took the magic out of it.
>
>Guy: OK, I'll cancel—
>
>Girl: NO!

25. If you drop your date off, wait until you see them get safely inside before leaving.

Guy: So wait, you want me to stare at you while you walk into your apartment and not leave until the door closes?

Girl: Yeah.

Guy: Doesn't that sound like crazy stalker stuff?

Girl: There's a fine line between considerate and stalker.

Guy: And you want me to do this naked, wrapped in Saran Wrap?

Girl: What? No. What just happened?

SARAN WRAP

26. Don't drive drunk. You could fucking die, you idiot.

Guy: Do we really have to have a conversation about this
    one?
Girl: Nah. We good.

27. Only kiss your date if you're sure they want to be kissed.

Guy: I have no idea if you want me to kiss you.
Girl: I have no idea if you want to kiss me.
Guy: So... should we talk about it?
Girl: That's super awkward.
Guy: Right.
    (They die alone.)
Dead Guy: What the fuck?
Dead Girl: You should've kissed me.

28. If you don't want to kiss your date, don't kiss them.

Girl: It was so nice to hang with you.
Guy: Likewise. Can I kiss you?
Girl: How about a super cool high-five?
Guy: I'm never gonna see you again, am I?
Girl: NOPE!

29. Don't drunk text after the date.

Girl's text: I had a fun time tonight.
Guy's drunk text: I want to munch on your titties like
Cookie Monster, gurrrl. NOM NOM
NOM.

(Girl throws out her phone.)

Following Up

30. The next day, shoot your date a text. Even if you don't have anything to say, just say "hi."

Guy's text: Hey, had fun last night.
Girl's text: Me too.
(Girl turns to a friend.)
Girl: He's obsessed with me.

WHAT IT LOOKS LIKE	WHAT IT FEELS LIKE

31. If you want to go on a second date with a person, schedule it ASAP.

Guy: Hey, I had a really good time, and I want to go out with you again, so I'm gonna wait five days then text "sup?"

Girl: Cool, I'm going to spend those five days wondering what went wrong and by the time you text I will hate you.

Guy: RELATIONSHIPS ARE SO FUN!

32. Don't play games. If you want to text someone, text them. If you want to call, call.

Guy: Hey, fun date yesterday.
Girl: I was going to text you this morning, but I didn't
      want to look desperate.
Guy: That's silly. Just text.
Girl: Why can't you text me first?
Guy: Why can't you text me first?
Girl: Why can't you?
Guy: Why can't you?
      (Etc. forever until the end of time.)

33. Put your phone down now.

Girl: Come on, put your phone down.

Guy: Sorry, I just got a message about my estranged father.

Girl: Oh, my God. I had no idea. My father abandoned my
     family too. I haven't seen him in years.

Guy: Oh no, sorry. "My Estranged Father" is the name of a
     band I'm seeing at 9:00 PM. I had a great convo with
     my pops this morning.

(Girl cries.)

(Guy puts phone down VERY gently.)

CHAPTER 4

TEXTING, APPS, AND OTHER INTIMACY-KILLING TECHNOLOGY

We know what you're thinking—first date went great, second date is set, now you can relax and rely on texting/social media to stay in touch. And of course you'd want to do that—everyone's life on the Internet looks awesome, but guess what, it's fake. So how about you get real for once and make a phone call? Yes, your phone can make phone calls. It's OK, we'll teach you everything.

Social Media

34. On social media, light stalking is expected but heavy stalking is creepy. Try to control yourself.

Girl: Hey, I followed you on Instagram last night.
Guy: I saw. You commented on every photo of mine that had a girl in it.
Girl: Yup.
Guy: Then you followed all of them.
Girl: Sure did.
Guy: I never want to see you again.
Girl: I'm impressed we made it this far.

35. Ask before posting a photo of the two of you together.

Guy: Nice to meet you.
   (Girl takes a selfie of the two of them and posts it on Instagram.)
Guy: Did you just post a photo of us? That's not cool.
Girl: It already has a hundred likes.
Guy: Tag me.

36. If you're not exclusive, don't tag your date on Instagram/ Twitter/Facebook.

Girl: This will make my ex so jealous!

Guy: It just seems too early to be tagging each other.

Girl: Why? Are you afraid some other girl you're dating is going to see it?

Guy: What?! No...*whaaat*? That's crazy...what?

Girl: I'll post it but not tag you, so she won't see.

Guy: Thank you.

37. Don't post on social media while you're on a date. Your incredible joke/photo can wait an hour.

> *(Girl Snapchats.)*
> Girl: Guys! I'm on a date and it's going TERRIBLE!
> *(Guy returns to the table.)*
> Guy: I follow you on Snapchat.

Texting

38. Don't read your date's texts.

Guy: There is literally no reason to read them. If you
     wanna know something, ask me.
     (Girl slowly backs away.)
Guy: You read my texts, didn't you?
     (Girl starts running away.)
Girl: Your mom wants you to come home more!

39. Reply to texts in a non-asshole amount of time.

Girl's text: What are you up to Fri?
...
...
...
Guy's text: Sorry, didn't have my phone on me.
Girl's text: I'm eighty years old now.

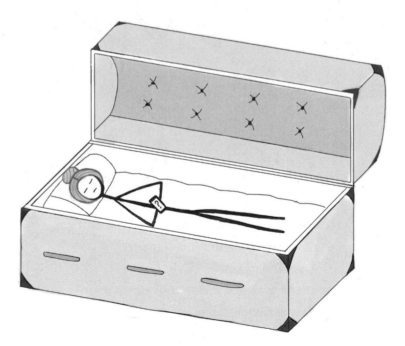

40. If someone doesn't text back in a timely manner, don't build a story in your head that they hate you/died/have a secret family.

Girl: Wow. It's been hours. Why hasn't he texted back? I bet he's on another date and on that date he ran into an ex and he was like "How's the dog?" and she's all "He misses you... actually, I miss you too." Then he says, "Why did we break up in the first place?" And she goes "I have no idea—BTW, are you dating anyone?" and he's like "NO, I LOVE YOU." Meanwhile, I'm just sitting here like a moron slowly dying alone... *(Girl's phone dings.)*

Guy's text: Was in a movie. 'Sup?

41. Using emojis and GIFs when you text can be fun. Using ONLY emojis and GIFs makes you look like a five-year-old. Stop it.

Guy: What does this text you sent last night mean? Girl waving hello, dragon, fire, wine, wine, wine, hospital mask, trash can, calendar.

Girl: It means "Hi, I'm watching *Game of Thrones* and drinking because I have my period and feel like garbage. Wanna hang later?"

Guy: Seriously? How do I write back "I don't think this is going to work"?

Girl: Hand waving, guy running, plane going up, sunset.

Guy: Thanks.

(Guy begins typing.)

42. Don't be afraid to leave a voicemail. It's like a text with words!

> *(Guy is on the phone.)*
> Guy: Shit! It's her voicemail. What if I say something dumb? Oh no, oh no, oh no. OK, you got this. Just be yourself.
> *(Voicemail beeps.)*
> Guy: *(in a cockney accent)* How them titties?
> *(Guy hangs up and pumps his fist.)*
> Guy: NAILED IT!!!

43. DO NOT send nude pics unless you're prepared for the consequences.

Girl: Why would you send me that?!

Guy: My dick looks ferocious.

Girl: You know I'm gonna show that to at least five friends, right?

Guy: Only five?

Dating Apps

44. Keep your "About Me" section short and sweet.

> Girl's profile: Hi! I've never done this before but here we go! I love ALL animals and pasta (for real!). My favorite city is Paris! Bonjour! And I'm looking to spend some quality time with someone kind, curious, and smokin' hot—jk!...sorta. LOL.
>
> Guy's profile: DTF.

45. Don't lie in your online profiles.

Girl: Umm, you're not what I expected.

Guy: I get that a lot. I guess I'm not exactly six-foot-four.

Girl: You are two children on top of each other in a trench coat.

Guy: Was that not on there? Weird. Waiter, I'd like two juice boxes please!

Girl: And the check!

46. Don't use douchey photos in your profile.

Guy: I think I'm good. I only have selfies of me on boats, in gyms, and next to women breast-feeding.
(Girl backs away and walks slowly into the ocean.)

47. Phone. Down. Now!

(Girl is on phone.)
Guy: PHONE.
Girl: But Insta—
Guy: DOWN.
Girl: But Snap—
Guy: NOW.
(Girl puts phone down.)

CHAPTER 5

SEX STUFF

Yes! You're about to be inside someone/let someone inside you! This is fucking insane! *Fucking* is insane! There's a lot to cover here— What's that? Oh, you're so good at sex you don't need our advice? OK, what about before and after the actual in-and-outing?...Exactly. Follow these tips to learn how to deal with the bookends of your gold medal fuck-fest.

General Sexing

48. Don't have sex with someone because you think you're supposed to. Have sex with someone because you want to.

> Guy: Listen, it's the third date, we're back at my place, and I get what's supposed to happen, but, honestly, if you don't want to have sex, I am totally cool with it.
>
> Girl: I'm good to go—
>
> *(Guy is instantly naked.)*

49. Don't expect sex, but be prepared for it.

Girl: Let's do it. Right here, right now!

Guy: What? Really? In this pet store?

Girl: You have a condom?

(Guy pulls a condom out of his hat.)

Girl: Wow.

Guy: I'm like an Eagle Scout but for boning.

50. Consent is simple. You know when you have it, and you
know when you don't have it.

Girl: Do we really have to have a conversation about this
    one?
Guy: Nah. We good.

51. If you're the one wearing the condom, you need to buy the condom.

>   Guy: What if we're at your place while it's all happening, and I don't have a condom?
>   Girl: Then we can use one of the leftover condoms in my nightstand.
>   Guy: I don't want to wear a "leftover condom" from some other dude.
>   Girl: THEN BUY YOUR OWN!

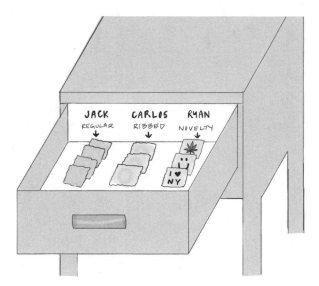

52. If you're the one using the morning-after pill, you do not buy the morning-after pill.

> Guy: WE HAVE TO BUY THIS, TOO?! It's so expensive!
> Girl: Google what happens to a girl's body when she takes the morning-after pill.
> *(Guy Googles "morning-after pill." Reads. Puts phone down.)*
> Girl: So?
> Guy: I'll pay for it.

53. Always reciprocate oral unless it's your birthday.

Girl: If I go down, you go down.
Guy: Like the *Titanic*?
Girl: Exactly. And if we do it right, neither of us will die.

54. SLOW DOWN. This isn't a race.

Girl: You remember the story of the Tortoise and the
      Hare? Where the Hare has sex so fast he tires out—
Guy: That's not how the story goes.
Girl: But the Tortoise goes slow and steady and wins by
      getting his girlfriend off.
Guy: Wait a second... is that how your parents told the
      story?
Girl: Of course. It's kind of similar to The Boy Who Cried
      Wolf—
Guy: Don't!

55. Start with the basics. Save the really insane moves for down
the road.

> *(Guy starts stretching.)*
> Guy: So I was thinking we'd start with a Sprawling Doris,
>   go into some Sweet Tarting, loop it around to a
>   Baked Alaska, and finish with a Santa's Goodbye—
> Girl: I was just gonna lie down…

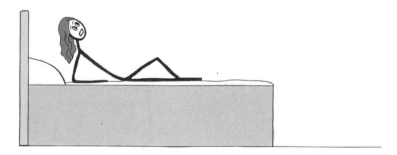

56. Talk about your weird fetish before you bust out your weird fetish. No one likes a sexual ambush.

Guy: Let's say our craziest fetish on the count of three.
Girl: OK. One, two, three...
Guy: Handcuffs.
Girl: I get myself off while you're wearing nothing but a mask of my face.
   (Beat.)
Guy: Wait, what?
Girl: I said handcuffs...

57. No one should be forced to cuddle, but at least hang out for a bit.

(Girl tries to cuddle Guy. Guy immediately moves away.)

Guy: I am so sorry but I'm allergic.

Girl: Allergic to cuddling?

Guy: Yeah, it makes my commitment issues flare up. Shit, it's happening right now.

Girl: You're an idiot.

Guy: The only antidote is blow jobs. You don't know where I can find one, do you?

Girl: Get out.

Sleepovers

58. If you're not sure you're coming back, don't borrow clothes. It's just going to cause you grief later.

Girl: Your T-shirt is so soft. Can I wear it home?
Guy: Sure, but I love that shirt, so you have to give it back.
Girl: I'm coming back?!
Guy: That's not what I meant.
Girl: Should I make a copy of your key?
Guy: Leave the shirt.

59. It's okay not to stay the night.

> Guy: Great sex. Wish I could stay but I have to go home
>   and walk my dog.
> Girl: You don't have a dog.
> Guy: I meant...hot dog.
> Girl: You have to go home and walk your hot dog?
> Guy: BYE!

60. PUT YOUR FUCKING PHONE DOWN, DUMB-DUMB!

Guy: I'm just checking the scores of—
    (Girl picks up his drink and crushes the glass in her hand.)
    (Guy puts phone down.)

CHAPTER 6

RELATIONSHIP STUFF

Oh no…you can't avoid it…WATCH OUT! IT'S COMING FOR YOU! COMMITMENT!!! After months of dating, it's time to choose between a relationship with one person or all the sex with everyone else. Yes, it could be scary, but it could also be amazing. So take our hand, pop a Xanax, and let us guide you through the horror that is feeling feelings.

Exclusivity

61. If you want to be exclusive with the person you are dating, TELL THAT PERSON!

Guy: Hey, I know this might be a little early but...what if we were exclusive?

Girl: Oh...like not date anyone else?

Guy: Yeah.

Girl: OK...I'm in.

(Guy smiles wide and hugs Girl.)

Girl: Fucking other people is still on the table, though, right?

Guy: What?! No.

Girl: I'm out.

62. Don't define the relationship over text. Use your mouth words.

Girl's text: (Guy raising hand emoji, heart emoji, girl raising hand emoji, dancing couple emoji, question mark.)
Guy's text: What?
Girl's text: (GIF of the kiss in the rain from *The Notebook*.)
Guy's text: Please use words.
Girl's text: Wanna b gf & bf?
Guy's text: I don't think my data plan can handle it.

63. When you decide to be exclusive, deactivate your dating apps/accounts.

Guy: Have you erased your dating apps?

Girl: Yep.

Guy: Oh, really? My friend said he matched with you yesterday.

Girl: Oh, I thought you said, "Have you erased your alley cats?"

Guy: What does that even mean?

Relationship Rules

64. Don't hide your significant other from your friends.

> Girl: I can't wait to meet your friends tonight! I'm so
> nervous!
> Guy: Don't stress. Just be yourself and you'll be great.
> Girl: Thanks. And just in case the conversation lags, I'm
> bringing my joke book.
> Guy: Please, for the love of God, leave the book at home.
> Girl: OK…I'll leave the book at home…
> *(Girl winks.)*

65. Give the other person's interests a shot.

> Girl: So we went to your improv theatre last night. Can I
>   pick what we do tonight?
> Guy: Absolutely. Which improv theatre do you want to go to?
> Girl: Oh, I was actually thinking something completely
>   different.
> Guy: A sketch show?
> Girl: No. Some place that has no comedy.
> Guy: I know just the place.
>   *(Guy takes Girl to his terrible open mic night.)*

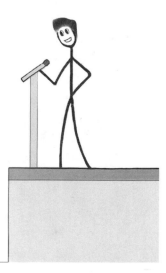

66. Keep your identity. You don't have to become your significant other. Retain your own interests.

Girl: I'm ready to go rock climbing with you.
Guy: You don't rock climb.
Girl: You kidding? Gonna slap my clampies on those rockers and shimmy up that hill.
Guy: None of that lingo is right.
Girl: Maybe for an amateur. Come on, grab your stompy boots and let's glide!

67. You are going to hate this, but if you're exclusively dating, you have to pick them up from the airport.

Girl: So, my flight arrives at 11:15.
Guy: PM?
Girl: Yep.
Guy: I kinda have an early morning the next day...
Girl: So?
Guy: I think we should take a break.

68. Just because you two are official doesn't mean you should coast.

Girl: How long have you been wearing those sweatpants?
Guy: Five perfect days.
Girl: Wow. That type of laziness is usually reserved for
      marriage. Are you saying you want to get married—
Guy: I'll get my jeans.

69. Don't lie and don't cheat.

Guy: Do we really need to talk about this one?

Girl: Nope. Seems straightforward to me.

Guy: Great.

Girl: Don't lie about your age and don't cheat on your diet.

Guy: No, don't lie to me or cheat on me.

Girl: Ohhhhhhhh.

Guy: Woof. OK, let's talk about this one.

Breaking Up

70. Don't be a ghost. Be a person.

Guy: I was thinking we should break up, but is it cool if
      instead of talking about it, I just gradually stop return-
      ing your calls and texts until you eventually have to
      prompt me into a conversation about what's happening?

Girl: Wow. Sounds really simple for you and an emotional
      mind fuck for me. Let's do it!

Guy: I knew you'd understand. I'll talk to you later. But...
      you know, not really.

71. Don't break up over text.

Girl: Wouldn't it be quicker for both of us if we broke up
over text?

Guy: Quicker, yes. But it would be mean.

Girl: Not really. This way I can write out exactly what I
want to say.

Guy: You can't say it to my face?

Girl: I don't want to see you hurt. I care about you.

Guy: THEN WHY ARE YOU BREAKING UP WITH
ME?!?

Girl: Read the text.

72. If someone is trying to break up with you, LET THEM.

Girl: I know you want to break up with me, but let's see how you feel after I cry, plead, and fake a pregnancy.
Guy: I would feel guilty enough to stay with you for a few months then gradually chip away at your self-confidence so when I get the courage to break up with you for real, you're a wreck and need years of therapy to get back on track.
Girl: I'm in.

73. You can stay friends with the person after you break up.

Guy: Let's stay friends, OK?
Girl: Absolutely. It's hard to find people you care about, so
    why would we throw that away?
Guy: Exactly. We can still hang out.
Girl: And kiss.
Guy: No. Not kiss. But we can be there for each other.
Girl: Naked.
Guy: You aren't getting this.

74. You did it! You put your phone down. DON'T YOU DARE PICK IT BACK UP!

Girl: OK, OK...so now that our phones are down, what
do we do?

Guy: Uh...

*(They sit there and stare at each other for ten seconds. It's
uncomfortable.)*

Guy: Siri, help me.

Siri: Don't drag me into this mess.

CHAPTER 7

LIVING SPACES

Now that you're in a relationship, you need to stop being such a selfish piece of shit. Your normal visiting hours of 2:00 AM to 9:00 AM now include all the other hours. You can't half-ass it anymore—it's time to put in actual effort and you know, go to their apartment every once in awhile. There's a lot of tricky shit here, but we got you. Take a seat, put your ringer on silent, and read about the secret world of pets, toothbrushes, and roommates.

At Your Place

75. Clean your room. Make your space presentable.

Girl: Wow, you cleaned the whole room for me.
Guy: Yup! It's just like you said, a guy with a clean room is
   a guy who's ready for an adult relationship.
   *(Girl opens the closet. A llama wearing a sombrero
   wanders out.)*
Girl: I'll show myself out.

76. Have an extra towel for them.

Girl: Can you hand me a towel?

Guy: Here, use mine.

Girl: It's damp. You just used it.

Guy: It's my only towel. Just use the dog.

Girl: Use the dog to dry myself off?

Guy: I mean, you can try the cat, but she's an asshole.

77. Have an extra toothbrush for them.

Guy: Why can't I just use yours?

Girl: That's disgusting. All of your teeth germs are on that.

Guy: So what? We've already swapped fluids.

Girl: We haven't rubbed teeth!

Guy: Not yet...

    (Guy walks over to Girl.)

Girl: NO!

At Their Place

78. Don't leave your stuff everywhere.

> *(Girl walks into room, trips over Guy's shoes.)*
> Girl: You can't just leave your shoes in the middle of the
>   room. One of us is going to get hurt.
> Guy: You told me to make myself comfortable.
> Girl: I meant make yourself comfortable in the neatest,
>   most non-invasive way possible.
> Guy: They're just shoes. It's fine.
> *(Guy walks out of room but trips over his shoes and dies.)*

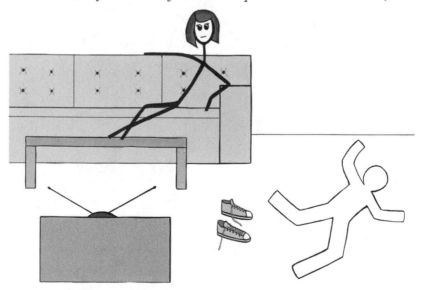

79. If you're constantly raiding their fridge, buy some shit to refill it.

Girl: Um, I can't find the leftovers.

Guy: Oh, wow, maybe someone robbed your apartment!

Girl: You think I got robbed and the only thing they took was General Tso's chicken?

Guy: You're also missing two beers and a pint of ice cream. You should get new locks.

(Girl stares at Guy. Guy picks up the phone.)

Guy: I'd like to place an order for delivery, please.

80. Be nice to their pets.

> Guy: I know you have a cat, but I'm allergic to cats, and also cats are horrible.
> Girl: Take a Claritin and cats are great.
> *(Beat.)*
> Guy: How long do cats live?
> Girl: Up to twenty years.
> Guy: And your cat is…nineteen?
> Girl: He's five.
> Guy: Cool. See you in fifteen years.

81. Be friendly to their roommates...but not too friendly.

Guy: Hey, roomie. Can I get your number? You know, for throwing surprise parties and other fun stuff?

Roommate: Sure.

(Roommate gives Guy the number.)

(Guy texts Roommate.)

Roommate: This is a photo of your penis.

Guy: Other fun stuff!

82. It's okay to take a shit at their place.

(Girl speaks through the bathroom door.)
Girl: You OK in there? It's been fifteen minutes.
Guy: Yep! Just…washing my hands.
Girl: Then why did you flush the toilet three times?
Guy: I was…checking your water pressure. It's good!
Girl: Just say you're shitting. It's okay.
Guy: I'M WASHING MY HANDS!

83. FOR THE LAST TIME. PUT. THE. FUCKING. PHONE. DOWN!!!

Guy: I DON'T WANT TO!
Girl: FUCK THIS! PICK ONE—ME OR THE PHONE!
Guy: . . . I mean, I just got the new iPhone.
Girl: AHHHHHHHHHH!!!

CHAPTER 8

THE FUTURE

You did it! By some miracle (this book, you're welcome), you turned a date into dating into a relationship. The only thing left to deal with is...the future. No, we don't mean hoverboards... we mean family holidays, moving in together, and...marriage. (If you just threw up on the book, clean it off before reading on.) Gather whatever strength you have left and get ready to stumble toward the future...which may or may not include hoverboards.

Friends/Family

84. Be nice to their friends. Even if you don't like them.

> Guy: Your friends are so annoying.
> Girl: You don't think I know that? Just hang in there and it'll be over soon.
> Guy: OK. But just so you know, you never have to talk to my friends.
> Girl: Oh, I would never talk to your friends.

85. Let them hang out with their friends without you.

Girl: Trust me, you'll be bored at ladies' night. We only talk about lipstick, tampons, and wage equality.

Guy: That actually sounds like fun. I'm in.

Girl: I lied. We're going to complain about our boyfriends, share all your secrets, and laugh at your fears.

Guy: Really?

Girl: No. But I just need time away from you sometimes.

Guy: It's cool. I can be alone. I'm definitely not afraid of being alone.

86. Be nice to their family.

Girl: Why won't you talk to my brother?

Guy: He's annoying.

Girl: Yeah, but he's family. Family is like an iCloud backup. If you get in, you get everything.

Guy: Do you even know how the iCloud works?

Girl: Of course not. No one does. Just be nice to my family.

Holidays

87. On Valentine's Day, remain calm and be clear about whether this holiday is important to you.

Guy: Are we doing gifts for V-Day?
Girl: I don't care, whatever you want.
Guy: OK, then let's skip it.
Girl: Cool.

    (Girl freezes her eggs.)

88. On Thanksgiving, don't get so drunk that you tell their family what you're *really* thankful for.

Drunk Guy: What up, dudes! Happy Pilgrim Hat Belt Day. Let me start this thanks train off— CHOO CHOO! I am thankful for this food, this wonderful family, and the fact your daughter doesn't have a gag reflex. LET'S EAT!

89. On Christmas/Chanukah/Kwanzaa, don't get so drunk that you can't convincingly pretend to love their gift.

Drunk Girl: I love it! What girl wouldn't want a...fart button? All of my friends are going to be super jealous 'cuz I know FOR A FACT none of them got fart buttons. They got stupid things like jewelry or Apple TVs. Here's your gift; it's a car. Sorry it doesn't fart.

90. On Flag Day...just treat this as a normal day.

> Girl: Happy Flag Day.
> Guy: Same. So...what happens now?
> Girl: Traditionally, the guy salutes the flag then goes down on his girlfriend.
> Guy: Incorrect.
> Girl: Worth a shot.

Special Occasions

91. If you're not serious about your partner, don't bring them as a plus one to a wedding.

> *(Girl holds up a brand new toaster.)*
> Girl: What's this for?
> Guy: That's for Danny's wedding. Wanna come with me?
> Girl: Are you asking me to be your date to Danny's wedding?
> Guy: Uh...sure.
> *(Girl cries and picks up her phone.)*
> Girl (on phone): Mom? He asked me to go to a wedding with him...AND I SAID YES! AHHHHH!!!
> Guy: I'm gonna take a bath.
> *(Guy takes the toaster and walks into the bathroom.)*

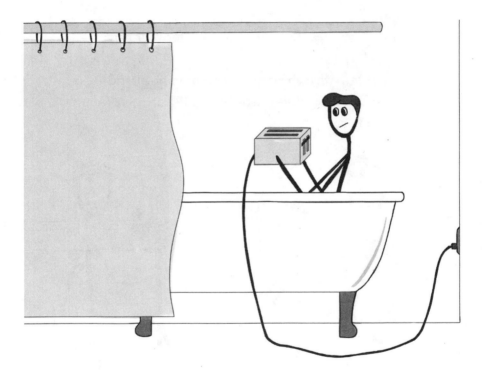

92. If you were the one invited to the wedding, you buy the gift.

> Girl: I'm gonna get them the expensive serving bowl set from their registry.
>
> Guy: Great idea! Go big or go home!
>
> Girl: Awesome. Can you Venmo me for your half?
> *(Beat.)*
>
> Guy: Or...what about getting them some plastic bags? Everyone needs plastic bags! I'll grab some from the kitchen.

93. Don't have sex at a funeral…unless the grieving person initiates.

Guy: I am so sorry for your loss.
> *(Guy kisses Girl on the cheek.)*

Girl: Thank you.
> *(Guy kisses Girl on the neck.)*

Girl: Um?
> *(Guy French kisses Girl.)*

Girl: What are you doing?!

Guy: Whoops. Misread some signals. My bad.
> *(Guy goes to his seat. Girl looks back at the crowd.)*

Girl (on microphone): Like I was saying…Grandpa Louie was a great man.

Moving in Together

94. Don't move in together too soon or for the wrong reasons.

> Girl: Living together is like...big-time adulting. Are you
> sure you're ready?
>
> Guy: Very sure. In fact...let's do it today 'cuz technically
> I'm getting "evicted" this afternoon. Which sucks
> because I also got "fired" this morning. You good to
> cover rent and utilities for the next six months?
>
> Girl: Umm...
>
> Guy: Great. Also, I just bought a snake. See ya soon!

95. Before you move in together, figure out how to split all the money stuff.

Guy: How about instead of splitting utilities fifty-fifty, whoever can do the most push-ups doesn't have to pay?

Girl: What? No.

Guy: Right, of course. How about whoever can eat the most hamburgers in an hour doesn't have to pay?

Girl: How about whoever gets all their pubic hair ripped off by hot wax every month doesn't have to pay?

Guy: Fifty-fifty sounds good.

96. When you move in together, remember that it's not just YOUR place anymore.

Girl: Why is there a workout bench in the bathroom?
Guy: I like to smash a quick pump before getting in the shower.
Girl: But it's blocking the way to the sink.
Guy: I don't see a sink. All I see are a billion beauty products.
> *(A beat. Girl takes products off the counter. Guy carries workout bench away. Girl puts products back.)*

Proposing

97. Get their parents' blessing before you propose. Or at the very least, give them a heads-up.

Guy: I'd like to marry your daughter.
Girl's Dad: Will you treat her well?
Guy: Yes, sir.
Girl's Dad: Will you get me a new TV?
Guy: Oh...I don't want to get you a new TV.
Girl's Dad: And I don't want you to have sex with my
daughter, but here we are. Your move, kid.

98. Propose in a location that's meaningful to both of you.

Girl: Where are we?

Guy: This is where I first knew I loved you.

Girl: I've never been here before.

Guy: I know. I was here banging someone else when I lost
    my boner and realized I only want to bang you.

(Guy gets down on one knee.)

Guy: Will you marry me?

(Girl puts on boxing gloves.)

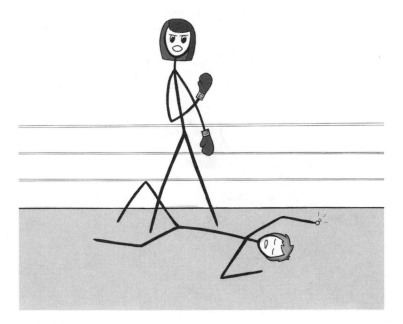

99. Don't let friends and family find out you're engaged through social media.

Girl: OMG! We have over a hundred likes on our ring pic!

Guy: I just got ten new followers!

Girl: We are nailing this engagement thing!

Guy: Your mom just commented, "You're engaged?!? Call me ASAP."

Girl: I'll DM her later.

100. ARE YOU SERIOUS?! YOU JUST GOT ENGAGED AND YOU'RE ALREADY ON YOUR PHONE?! WE GIVE UP. YOU TWO SHOULD MARRY YOUR PHONES.

CONCLUSION

Hooray! You made it to the end! You are probably exhausted, but we wanted to say one last thing before you passed out: we're proud of you. Seriously. We know how hard it is to leave your apartment, meet someone, listen to their words, go to their apartment, meet their friends, have good sex, pet their cat, and settle down. Even if you screwed up everything and everyone hates you, at least you tried. Putting yourself out there is the hardest part of this whole thing, so give yourself a pat on the back and once you're ready— get back out there again. Don't worry, if it doesn't work out you'll always have your phone, you adorable fucking idiot.

ACKNOWLEDGMENTS

We would like to thank our editor Lauren Hummel, publisher Mauro DiPreta, as well as Kara Thornton, Odette Fleming, Carlos Esparza, Melanie Gold, and Melissa Mathlin at Hachette Books for helping us turn this weird idea into an actual book. A huge thank you to our agent, Jud Laghi; manager, Rachel Miller; and everyone at Haven for their guidance, encouragement, and assortment of snacks. We'd also like to thank...um...

Guy: Wow, is that it?

Girl: I feel like other book acknowledgments are way longer than this.

Guy: Who else do we know?

Girl: Our families!

Guy: They didn't help us write the book.

Girl: We just need to fill space.

Guy: OK, thanks to our families and...um...

Girl: Big shout-out to my cats!

Guy: They will never know you thanked them.

Girl: Oh, Arlo and Poppy will know.

Guy: Wow.

Girl: I'd like to thank all my exes: Drew, Paul, Jon, Jesse, Michael, another Michael, Elliot...

Guy: You went out with Elliot?

Girl: It was a dark time.

Guy: But I mean, ELLIOT?!?

Girl: Whatever. Anyone else you want to thank?

Guy: Steven Spielberg.

Girl: It never hurts to thank Steven Spielberg.

Guy: Oooh! And ice cream.

Girl: You're lactose intolerant.

Guy: It's a love/hate relationship.

Girl: We should probably thank the person who's reading this right now. Thank you, wonderful human, for buying our book!

Guy: What if they're just reading it in the bookstore or on some website and they didn't actually buy it?

Girl: Who picks up a book in a bookstore and immediately reads the acknowledgments?

Guy: Elliot would.

Girl: Shut up.

Guy: OK, is this part long enough now?

Girl: It's perfect. We come off as total pros.

ABOUT THE AUTHORS

Ben Schwartz is an Emmy Award–winning writer, actor, and comedian. He's starred in the television shows *House of Lies* and *Parks and Recreation* as well as the films *This Is Where I Leave You* and *The Walk*. He is the co-author of the national bestseller *Grandma's Dead: Breaking Bad News with Baby Animals* and its two sequels.

Laura Moses is an Emmy Award–less writer for both film and television, whose credits include *Married* on FX and several animated feature films. She is the co-author of the soon-to-be national bestseller *Things You Should Already Know About Dating, You F*cking Idiot*. In her spare time, she enjoys yoga, volunteering, and reading Ben's bio.

YOUR TURN

Did we miss something? Chances are, you've had some crazy experiences that we didn't cover in the book. It's time to help out your fellow idiots. Write your own tips, explain them in a conversation, and illustrate them on the following pages. Then send us pics of your tips and illustrations on social media so we can all learn/silently judge.

101.

102.